S0-BIM-440

PAUL TILLICH

by

J. HEYWOOD THOMAS

JOHN KNOX PRESS
RICHMOND, VIRGINIA

British edition published by Lutterworth Press,
London, England, 1965

American edition published by John Knox Press, Richmond,
Virginia, 1966

Standard Book Number: 8042-0678-3
Library of Congress Catalog Card Number: 66-11072
Printed in the U.S.A.

Sixth printing 1969

Contents

I

Life

THE last years of the nineteenth century saw the birth of three leading theologians of our day – Barth, Brunner and Tillich. Paul Tillich was born on 20 August, 1886, the son of a Lutheran clergyman, in Starzeddel, a village in the province of Brandenburg. He has emphasised the importance of the fact that he was born in the nineteenth century, and there is no doubt that his early years have profoundly influenced his development. These influences have often been conflicting. Tillich speaks of himself as living on the boundary between two temperaments, that of the Rhineland inherited from his mother and that of Prussia inherited from his father. His father was very conservative and nurtured in the boy a respect for tradition whereas the mother encouraged the liberal adventurous tendencies of the youthful enquiring mind. Born in a rural area Tillich has always felt himself strongly attached to the country. His appreciation of nature is such that he has been prepared to accept the label of 'romantic'. As Leibrecht says, 'Let him but speak of a tree and his romantic strain at once becomes apparent.'[1] This romantic attitude toward nature was strengthened by his reading of the German poets and also by his experience of life in the sleepy beautiful towns where he spent his earliest childhood. All this, Tillich freely admits, influenced his development as a theologian. But if this attachment to the land and to the past tended to make him something of a traditionalist the other influence was also very active. Besides his memories of the soil, weather, wind and woods there are his memories of visiting the strangely exciting big city, Berlin, and of his life there as a young man.

[1] W. Leibrecht, 'The Life and Mind of Paul Tillich', in W. Leibrecht (ed.), *Religion and Culture*, New York and London, Harper and S.C.M. Press, 1959, p. 7.

When Paul was only fourteen his father was called to a position in Berlin, and this pleased the lad immensely. By this time he was in a grammar school and he continued his classical studies in Berlin, matriculating in 1904. In University he read philosophy and theology, taking the degrees of Doctor of Philosophy of Breslau and of Licentiate of Theology of Halle. In 1912 he was ordained to the ministry of the Evangelical Lutheran Church in the province of Brandenburg. Two years later the First World War broke out, and Tillich joined the army as chaplain.

The war years were very important years in Tillich's development, and to them may be traced the rise of two of his greatest interests – his interest in art and his interest in politics. The ugly gruesomeness and destructiveness of war drove him to seek relief and he found it in painting. He studied reproductions of paintings and he read deeply in the history of art. This adventure reached its climax during his last leave of the war when he visited Berlin and saw a picture by Botticelli there. This interest in art has profoundly influenced Tillich's thought in various directions. It was from reflection upon his experience of art and its interpretation that he derived the fundamental categories of his philosophy of religion. It was this too that first set him thinking about a theology of culture. In a sense his theology as a whole is concerned with the theology of culture because it is self-consciously open to contemporary culture; but in the narrower sense of being concerned with specific aspects of contemporary culture Tillich's lectures from 1919 to 1924 were lectures on the theology of culture. This was his attempt at producing an apologetic theology which would speak to the cultural upheaval of post-war Berlin. Yet another contribution of the war period to Tillich's development was his conversion (if this is the right word) to Socialism. After a few months as a chaplain on the western front the early enthusiasm of 'the overwhelming experience of a nation-wide community' was lost and Tillich felt that 'the war would last indefinitely and ruin all Europe'.[2] The apparent unity of the nation was an illusion. What was worse was that in the class

[2] *Theology of Paul Tillich*, p. 12.

struggle the church was regarded as an ally of the ruling groups. Tillich had always been sympathetic to social struggle. Now he saw that this had to be expressed openly or the Christian minister was regarded as an enemy of the social revolution. Tillich became an ardent advocate of religious socialism. Though born into the bourgeoisie he had himself not become bourgeois because he had contact with all classes. Now he felt drawn by the reforming aims of the Socialist movement though he did not share the naïve utopianism of so many of his contemporaries. So he stood on the boundary between idealism and Marxism in philosophy and in the world of affairs on the boundary between Lutheranism and Socialism. He did not identify himself with the Socialist Party and says that he has never belonged to any political party. Even so he published a small work on Socialism in 1933 called *Die sozialistische Entschedung*, and when later the editor of *The Christian Century* gave an article of his the title 'Beyond Religious Socialism' he was very cross, remarking that if the prophetic message is right, then there can be nothing 'beyond' religious Socialism.

Apart from one year teaching theology at Marburg (1924–25) the nineteen-twenties were spent by Tillich teaching philosophy in the Universities of Dresden, Leipzig and Frankfurt. Though it was only a year he spent there, Marburg has left its mark on Tillich. There he met with existentialism in its twentieth-century form. His reaction he describes thus: 'I resisted, I tried to learn, I accepted the new ways of thinking more than the answer it gave.' In some ways it was not a new way of thinking – at any rate, Tillich regards himself as having been prepared for it by three things – his familiarity with Schelling, his knowledge of Kierkegaard and the contact he had had with 'the philosophy of life'. Certainly his teaching of philosophy in Dresden was designed to make philosophy a live issue for his pupils, and his lectures were concerned with the boundary between philosophy and theology. Professional philosopher though he was, Tillich regarded himself as a theologian: 'I was and I am a theologian, because the existential question of our ultimate concern and the existential answer of the Christian message are and always have been predominant in my spiritual life.'[3] Tillich's sympathies in theology were clearly with the new 'dialectical' theology which had been pioneered by Karl Barth, and his early work is full of Barthian ideas. Like Barth, he insists on Kierkegaard's 'infinite qualitative difference' between the temporal and the eternal, on the necessity of revelation and the inevitability of paradox when human language tries to express the divine revelation. However, Tillich was too liberal-minded to follow Barth entirely, and increasingly his work became sharply distinguished from 'dialectical theology'. His strictures on Barth's theology reached a climax in his article, 'What is wrong with the "Dialectic" Theology?' which was published in the *Journal of Religion* in 1935, and he has argued that this theology is indeed opposed to any kind of dialectics.

As a result of his condemnation of National Socialism in his writing and public speaking Tillich lost his chair in the University of Frankfurt. Through the efforts of the Niebuhr brothers he emigrated to the United States of America and became Professor of Philosophical Theology at Union Theological Seminary, New York. His sturdy figure was well known on Morningside Heights as he made his way back and fore from Union Seminary to Columbia University. From 1933 to 1955 he taught in New York, and in 1955 he moved on to Harvard to become University Professor. From Harvard he has gone to Chicago where once more hundreds of students eagerly fill the largest of lecture-rooms to listen to his lectures. Not only the greater part of his academic career has been spent in the United States but also, whilst there, he has published most of his books. The great output was crowned in 1963 by the publication of the final volume of *Systematic Theology*.

[3] *Theology of Paul Tillich*, p. 10.

2

Thought

As we have seen, Tillich has been active in various fields and can be studied for his value as a philosopher and a political thinker as well as for his value as a theologian. Whilst this, like any account of his thought, must take note of the work he has done in the fields of philosophy and political theory, mostly we shall be concerned with Tillich's theology.

Liberal Roots

The liberal roots of Tillich's theology are very evident. His theology, he tells us, is apologetic and will be 'carried through in a continuous correlation with philosophy'.[4] A theological system has two poles – tradition and the present situation. It serves the two different functions of stating the truth of the Christian message and of interpreting this truth for every generation. Unless devotion to the tradition is completed by apologetics which speak to the special situation in which the theologian finds himself his theology will become a rigid, narrow and irrelevant orthodoxy. On the other hand if apologetic theology is to retain its special Christian character it must be 'based on the *kerygma* as the substance and criterion of each of its statements'. Tillich's aim in his theology is to combine these two elements. Thus, though his theology is essentially apologetic he is so impressed by the *kerygmatic* character of theology that he insists that the theologian must work within 'the theological circle'. This is what distinguishes the theologian's task from that of the philosopher of religion.

Tillich recognises two formal criteria of every theology. The

[4] *Systematic Theology*, i, London, Nisbet, pp. ix–x. Afterward referred to as *S.T.*

first is that only those propositions are theological which deal with their object in so far as it can become a matter of ultimate concern for us. The second formal criterion of every theology is that only those statements are theological which deal with their object in so far as it is a matter of being or not being for us. The norm of theology is best expressed: 'the New Being in Jesus as the Christ as our ultimate concern'.[5] Clearly then, Tillich will not want to start with a natural theology. Indeed he wants to replace the traditional distinction between natural and revealed theology by an incorporation of the philosophical element in natural theology into the structure of the system itself, using it as the material out of which questions are developed. Similarly he suggests that apologetics should not be regarded as a separate element of theology but should rather be regarded as an ever-present element of systematic theology. Finally, no more than apologetics should moral theology be made a special section of theology. An existential theology necessarily implies ethics and so no separate moral theology can be admitted: in every theological statement the ethical is not only a necessary but often the fundamental element.

Tillich rejects the neo-orthodox view that the Bible is the *only* source of systematic theology and he argues that the biblical message could not have been received had there not been preparation for it in human history. Since, therefore, the biblical message embraces more than the biblical books systematic theology has other sources besides the Bible. Yet the Bible, Tillich admits, is the basic source of systematic theology because it is the 'original document' about the events on which the Christian church is founded. The biblical material is made available as a source of systematic theology by the biblical theologian who is concerned not with pure historical fact but with 'theologically interpreted facts'. In so far as the Bible is an event in church history the systematic theologian implicitly uses church history when he uses the Bible. He must do this explicitly as well as implicitly. Together with church history there is another historical source of systematic theology – the history of reform and culture. The

[5] *S.T.*, i, p. 50.

medium through which we receive these sources is 'experience'. There are, says Tillich, three uses of this word – the ontological, the scientific and the mystical. The real problem for empirical theology is experience in the sense of mystical experience. Here the danger is that of asserting that the source of systematic theology is a religious experience which transcends the Christian message as bound to the unique event of Jesus the Christ. Christian theology, says Tillich, 'is based on the unique event of Jesus the Christ',[6] and this event is given to experience and not derived from it.

This account of the sources of systematic theology has been criticised very effectively by Catholic theologians, notably Fathers Dulles and Tavard.[7] Father Dulles argues that in his handling of the Bible Tillich tends to 'overlook the divine element in holy scriptures and in effect denies that it is the word of God'. Further he maintains that Tillich 'unduly minimises the historical elements in the Bible' whilst solemnly affirming that 'there was a Jesus who lived on earth and spoke with his disciples'. Father Tavard criticises Tillich's understanding of the rôle of experience in systematic theology, finding in it an inconsistency which takes us to the heart of Tillich's theology. For Tillich experience is the medium through which we receive the theology, but it is not itself a source of theology: its productive power is limited to the transformation of what is given to it. But this transformation is also described as something required by the message or something that is necessary for its adequate presentation. How far, then, asks Father Tavard, can we say that experience is not productive? Again, the New Being itself is mediated through the theologian's experience. How far does this mediating experience transform it? Father Tavard feels that Tillich's new path in theology is that of reducing the dichotomy between subject and object, but this, despite the fact that it is essential to Tillich's understanding of faith is, not a distinctly Christian phenomenon.

[6] *Op. cit.*, p. 52.
[7] See my *Paul Tillich: An Appraisal*, London, S.C.M. Press, pp. 188 ff.

Method of Theology

Two things must be said about the method of theology, according to Tillich. It is rational and it is a method of correlation. There are three senses of the word 'rational' in which it is true to say that theology is rational – the semantic, the logical and the methodological. He does not make quite clear what he means by the demand for semantic rationality. Certainly he means that the theologian must elucidate what he means, but he seems to think that this can only be done in so far as the theologian consciously relates all the connotations of a word to each other and centres them around a 'controlling meaning'. Theology is also rational in the sense of being logical. Theology, says Tillich, is as dependent on formal logic as any other science. The point of this remark is not only that the argument of the theologian must be sound according to the rules of logic but more especially that the paradoxes which the theologian must of necessity employ are without exception 'existential and not logical'; that is, they are not logical contradictions. Finally, theology is rational in so far as it is methodical and therefore systematic. Once you start on the task of theological reflection you must carry it through consistently and rationally – which means, says Tillich, that you form a system. Theology is both *kerygmatic* and apologetic and so the method it must employ, says Tillich, is the method of correlation. This method, he says, 'explains the contents of the Christian faith through existential questions and theological answers in interdependence'.[8] The analysis of the 'situation' is the work of the philosopher. Philosophy asks questions to which theology provides the answers. This is why the method of correlation often seems to be Tillich's answer to the question of the relation between philosophy and theology rather than the general characterisation of the method theology employs. Its success as an answer to this problem derives from the way in which Tillich defines both philosophy and theology. Philosophy, he says, is that cognitive science in which reality as such is the object. It asks the ultimate

[8] *S.T.*, i, p. 68.

question 'as to what being, simply being, means'.[9] Theology also asks the question of reality as a whole, for only that which belongs to reality as a whole can concern us ultimately. In so far as any philosophy has an existential concern it carries within itself either a hidden or an acknowledged theology. The questions Tillich has answered are fundamental questions for every theologian, and so the fact that they are open to severe criticism does not mean that these answers are unimportant. I have myself raised two main questions[10] which have in different ways been raised by other critics. The first is that the whole discussion of the rationality of theology presupposes some kind of formalism both in theory of language and in the understanding of theological argument. Putting the matter baldly we can say that Tillich is guilty of thinking that the meaning of language is some peculiar entity which is indissolubly linked to language itself and that his formalist outlook leads him to force theological argument into the Procrustean bed of formal logic. The other point is that the correlation of philosophy and theology fails to do justice either to philosophy or to theology. It could even be said that he allows his conception of philosophy to determine the nature of theology. No amount of protesting that the content of the theological answer is given in revelation can remove the offence of regarding theology as having merely the value of providing us with the answers to *our* questions instead of being the light that lightens our feet so that even the question is given. This has been argued by more than one Catholic critic[11] and Kenneth Hamilton's book *The System and the Gospel* makes this its central thesis.

Revelation

According to his own method of correlation Tillich's starting-point in theology must be the question developed by an analysis of the human situation. So he begins by analysing man's cogni-

[9] *Protestant Era*, p. 95.
[10] See *Paul Tillich: An Appraisal*, pp. 27–45.
[11] Cf. *ibid.*, pp. 189 ff.

tive situation, his cognitive rationality and the question implied in the ambiguities of reason. Then he seeks to force the answer to this question, namely Revelation. Tillich distinguishes several concepts of reason, of which the most important here are 'the depth of reason' and 'ecstatic reason'. The depth of reason 'is the expression of something that is not reason, but which precedes reason and is manifest through it'.[12] What exactly this is we are never told, but it may be a kind of intuitive union with reality which under the conditions of human cognition we cannot have. At any rate Tillich sees in reason a conflict between the demand for detachment and the demand for intuitive union with the object of our knowledge. Again we ask ourselves whether we can by our own thinking know anything about reality. Here clearly we meet the idea of revelation. Revelation is the occurrence of an event which evokes 'numinous astonishment'. This experience is the state of 'ecstasy', a state of reason in which reason transcends its normal subject-object structure. The ecstatic reason is the subjective side of a situation in which some event occurs which evokes it and which we may then call a 'sign event'. The occurrence of this whole situation is revelation. Tillich distinguishes between original and dependent revelations.[13] An original revelation 'is a revelation which occurs in a constellation that did not exist before'. This miracle and this ecstasy are joined for the first time. In a dependent revelation the two factors are not pure miracle on the one hand and pure ecstatic reception on the other but are the original miracle, together with its original reception, on the one hand, and on the other, a variable factor which changes as new individuals and groups receive the revelation. There is continuous revelation in the history of the church, but it is dependent revelation. Whether it is original or dependent, revelation has revelatory power only for those who participate in it. History has shown, says Tillich, how a revelatory correlation came to an end by a complete disappearance of the unchanging point of reference or by a complete loss of its power to create new revelatory situations. Knowledge gained from revelation adds

[12] *S.T.*, i, p. 88. [13] *S.T.*, i, pp. 140–42.

nothing to knowledge about the structure of nature, history and man.[14] Knowledge of revelation is knowledge about the revelation of the mystery of being and not information about the nature of beings and their relation to one another. For this reason it is also true that ordinary empirical knowledge cannot interfere with revelatory knowledge. However, we must remember that within ordinary knowledge there are revelatory elements and so this independence can never be complete. Theology must always be prepared to protect the truths of revelation against attack even if the attack should be made under the guise of ordinary knowledge.

Some of the criticisms that can be levelled against this interpretation of revelation will be mentioned when we examine Tillich's christology. However, there is one that can be mentioned now. Tillich regards the Christian revelation as absolute and as such, he says, it includes the criterion of every revelation. This would suggest that the notion of revelation transcends Christianity. Now some theologians would insist that however true it is that there is revelation outside the Christian tradition, that at no time has God left himself without witness, yet in Christian theology the term 'revelation' means the fact that God has now spoken to us in his son. In other words, the term 'revelation' is for the Christian theologian synonymous with 'Jesus Christ'. So the criticism becomes even an argument *ad hominen* in so far as Tillich insists that the new being is the norm of theology. According to this criticism, his theology is not sufficiently christocentric.

The Idea of God

Though Tillich begins by talking of revelation and the holy, he soon turns his attention to the idea of God. God, he tells us, is that which ultimately or unconditionally concerns us.[15] This is Tillich's philosophical translation of the first commandment: 'Thou shalt love the Lord thy God with all thy heart.' Without referring to our religious life, all we can say of God is the bare

[14] *Ibid.*, p. 143. [15] *Ibid.*, p. 14.

assertion that God is 'being itself' or 'the power of being whereby it resists non-being'. All descriptions of God other than this are symbolical and not literal. Properly to understand this doctrine of Tillich's we must first of all appreciate that he does admit some exceptions to this general rule that all statements about God are symbolical and secondly we must understand what he means by a symbol. First he often speaks as if terms such as eternity, absolute and unconditioned were synonymous with being itself.[16] He also raises the question of a non-symbolic anchor to the symbolical language[17] and contends that this is found in the statement of his general rule. That is, the one non-symbolic assertion about God which the symbolical requires is the assertion that everything that we say about God is symbolical. It has been pointed out how Tillich has here succumbed to a popular logical fallacy inasmuch as the assertion question is not about God. Secondly, Tillich often insists that we should never talk of 'mere symbols'. Symbols are not mere signs but, unlike signs, participate in the reality or in the power of that to which they point. In a discussion with one of his most distinguished critics, the late Father Weigel, he said that what he meant by 'symbol' was what Aquinas meant by 'analogy'. Other critics, as well as Father Weigel, have pointed out not only the error of such a description but also the inadequacy of Tillich's doctrine of symbols.

To return to our exposition of Tillich's doctrine of God let us see what the symbolical descriptions are. Central ones are that he is 'living' and 'personal', that he is 'the creative and abysmal ground of being' and that he is 'spirit' or 'love'. Life is 'the process in which potential being becomes actual being'; but, since God transcends the distinction between potential and actual, God is 'not living in the proper or non-symbolic sense'. God is living in so far as he is the ground of life. 'Ground' does not here mean 'cause' or 'substance' taken literally but something which underlies all things in some way or other which we can describe only by means of some such symbol as cause. God is not a thing or an object; he has selfhood. But self implies 'separation from and

[16] Cf. *S.T.*, i, pp. 217, 265, 304. [17] *S.T.*, ii, p. 10.

contrast to everything which is not self' whereas God, since he is being-itself, is separate from nothing. He is super-personal but we necessarily speak of him symbolically as personal.[18] God is free and yet he has a destiny – again in a non-literal sense, since in God destiny is 'an absolute and unconditional identity' with freedom. In no sense can we say that God exists because existence necessarily implies being subject to space, time and causality.[19] The medieval theologians who argued about the proof of God's existence were not arguing about the same thing – 'the one group did not attack what the other group defended'. In any case, the notion of an argument for God's existence is fallacious on two counts. 'Both the concept of existence and the method of arguing to a conclusion are inadequate for the idea of God.' Tillich repudiates this method because he says it must derive the idea of God from the world so that God is 'world', a missing part of that from which we derive our conclusion. This means that God cannot be what transcends the world infinitely. The classical proofs then are neither proofs of, nor arguments for, the existence of God. They are expressions of the *question* of God which is implied in human finitude. The ontological argument is an analysis of the human situation which shows that the question of God is possible and the two cosmological arguments show that the question of God is necessary.

Several critics have argued that Tillich's treatment of the existence of God is inadequate. The obvious advantages of repudiating the concept of existence are more than balanced by the difficulties in which he involves himself. Even those who do not wish, as Catholic theologians do, to maintain that there are valid proofs of the existence of God would want to say that somehow we must say that God exists. The interpretation of the classical arguments is artificial and inadequate. There is a sense in which what these arguments say is true. That is, if they are used cautiously they can both express religious awareness and evoke it. As for the doctrine of God as a whole, its apparent agreement with classical doctrine has not dissuaded critics from questioning

[18] *S.T.*, i, p. 271. [19] *Ibid.*, p. 227.

its fidelity to the classical tradition. When God does not exist, is being-itself and has a dialectical negativity within himself, is this still the God of Abraham?

The doctrine of God receives further elaboration in *The Courage to Be* where Tillich reaches the conclusion that the courage of the Reformation, the courage of confidence, 'transcends both the courage to be as a part and the courage to be as oneself'.[20] It is based on God, on God alone, and he is experienced in a unique and personal encounter. In its centre is 'the courage to accept acceptance in spite of the consciousness of guilt'.[21] The experience of the power of being which is effective in every act of courage is faith, and faith is paradoxical in character. It is accepting and being accepted, accepting acceptance. Faith accepts the fact that he who is separated is accepted. To the question whether faith can resist meaninglessness Tillich answers that there is a faith which makes 'the courage of despair' possible, and this is 'absolute faith'.[22] Absolute faith transcends the theistic idea of God. What is wrong with 'theological theism' is that it conceives of God as 'a being beside others and as such a part of the whole of reality'. Absolute faith requires the idea of a God above God, the God that becomes manifest when the God of theism has died.

We have seen how Tillich regards God as the ground of being, the creative ground of all that exists. God is creative because he is God,[23] and so it is meaningless, says Tillich, to ask whether creation is a necessary or a contingent act of God. Creation is identical with God's life. It is not a story of an event which took place once upon a time. 'It is the basic description of the relation between God and the world.' This is symbolised by talking of creation as having taken place, as taking place and as the future fulfilment of God's *telos* (originating creation, sustaining creation and directing creation). The classical Christian doctrine of creation is expressed by the formula *creatio ex nihilo*, and the first thing we must do is to understand what this means. First of all, it rejects any kind of dualism such as was found in pagan thought.

[20] *The Courage to Be*, p. 155.
[21] *Ibid.* [22] *Ibid.*, p. 167. [23] *S.T.*, i, p. 280.

God has nothing presented to him which either assists or hinders creativity. But there is more than this in the formula because the word 'ex' points to the origin of the created – it comes from nothing. So the formula means for Tillich that there is in the creature 'the heritage of non-being'.[24] This means two things. First, it means that the tragic character of existence is not rooted in the creative ground of being and so does not belong to the essential nature of things. Secondly, though the tragic is not necessary it is potential. Symbolising this originating creativity of God as we do by speaking of it as a past event, we are instantly faced with the question, what did God do before he created the world? This question Tillich regards as being both philosophically absurd and religiously repugnant, and the answer to it must be sought in our understanding of the creative character of the divine life. If it is true that creativity is essential to the divine life then it is true that the forms of finitude (and not just the finite itself) are in some sense present in that life. So the divine life includes temporality. God's eternity is not opposed to time but includes it and transcends it. Tillich rejects any deistic understanding of the preservation of the world and adopts the Augustinian view of the preservation as continuous creation. However, he wants to develop this view of preservation into an attack on the idea of God as a being alongside the world. Finally, in talking of God's directing creativity Tillich prefers to speak of the *telos* of creation, for he insists that creation has no purpose beyond itself. The divine creativity drives every creature toward the fulfilment in actuality of what is beyond potentiality and actuality in the divine life. This is traditionally called 'providence'. Faith in providence is always paradoxical in that it asserts that things are not what they seem. In spite of the incessant experiences of meaninglessness it asserts that historical existence has meaning. This, however, is not to believe that a special divine activity will alter the conditions of finitude. Faith in historical providence means that we are certain that all history contributes to the ultimate fulfilment of creaturely existence.

[24] *Ibid.*, p. 281.

The Incarnation

This exposition of Tillich's doctrine of God enables us now to understand the way he has reinterpreted the doctrine of incarnation. To call Jesus the Christ meant for the disciples, says Tillich, that with him the new aeon would come about and that he would inaugurate a new state of things.[25] This expectation was not fulfilled in accordance with the disciples' hopes. This meant that they had either to abandon their hopes or radically change their content. This change of content was effected by the identification of the New Being with the sacrificed Christ. The New Being in Jesus as the Christ is expressed in his whole being, and neither his words nor his deeds nor his sufferings nor yet his 'inner life' make him the Christ. These are all expressions of the New Being which is the quality of his being. Tillich says that his use of the term 'New Being' in relation to Jesus is analogous to his use of the term 'Being' in his doctrine of God. When applied to Jesus as the Christ, the term 'New Being' points to the power in him which conquers existential estrangement. In the biblical picture of Christ three things are emphasised: the complete fortitude of the Christ, the reality of the temptations arising out of it, and finally the victory over these temptations.[26] The picture of the New Being in Jesus as the Christ is not then a picture of a divine automaton, for none of life's ambiguities is removed in his existence and he faces serious temptation and real struggles. The picture we have is that of a personal life in which all the ambiguities of life are transcended in permanent unity with God.

It will be seen that Tillich bases his christology on what he has called the picture of Christ which we have in the New Testament. In this way he has tried to rid theology of the confusions that have arisen as a result of the ambiguous expression, 'the historical Jesus'. This expression can be used to mean either the historical evidence concerning Jesus or the factual character of the event, 'Jesus as the Christ'. It is this ambiguity, says Tillich, which blinds us to the obvious impossibility of giving a foundation to

[25] *S.T.*, ii, pp. 135 ff. [26] *Ibid.*, p. 146.

the Christian faith through historical research. On the question of 'an actual historical Jesus' Tillich makes some five points. First, the incarnation was a fact which could have been in theory recorded as neutral evidence. In fact, of course, we do not have such a photographic record of his existence; but this does not minimise its factuality. Secondly, though we do not have a photograph, we do have a portrait. This man is portrayed in the New Testament as Jesus who is the Christ, the Son of God, the Logos. Thirdly, the quest of historical criticism yields, like all historical inquiry, only a high degree of probability. The historian can never reach certainty, and this is not enough for faith. Its certainty cannot rest upon a probability. So the history of the revelation is a matter of the immediate certainty of faith. Fourthly, the historicity of the revelation portrayed in the New Testament means not only that such a person as Jesus did exist but also that he was such as to support the biblical picture. Finally, the certainty given by faith comes to the Christian in an experience which has two aspects. It is his as a member of the church which is the actual continuation of the history of revelation, and secondly it is his as an individual grasped by the revealing event. Though historical criticism cannot thus yield a basis for the Christian faith, it is relevant to christological doctrine in three ways. First, it helps the theologian understand the christological symbols of the Bible. Secondly, historical research shows how the biblical authors developed the implications of their sharing in the revelation and indirectly contributes to the same development in the critic. Finally, the theologian will be helped in his attempt at a new correlation of faith and culture by examining that which is found in the Bible.

Two questions can be asked, says Tillich, about the christological dogma: 1. What measure of success did it have in the task of preserving the Christian message against distortion? 2. How successful was the conceptualisation of the symbols expressing the Christian message? Tillich's answer is that the christological dogma saved the church but with very inadequate tools.[27] The

[27] *Ibid.*, p. 167.

inadequacy of the tools is due not only to the inevitable inadequacy of any concept to express the New Being in Jesus and the Christ, but also to the dependence of the Greek concept upon a concrete religion determined by the divine figure of Apollos and Dionysius. The doctrine of the two natures leads to absurd conclusions, as liberalism revealed, and so Tillich thinks it should be replaced by the 'dynamic-relational concepts' of 'eternal God-man-unity' or 'eternal God-Manhood'.[28] It might be thought that this substitution involves Tillich in an adoptionist christology. Tillich raises this question himself and answers it with two points. First, an adoptionist christology has biblical roots just as much as an incarnational christology has. Secondly, neither of them can be fully stated without implying the other.

It would be as well to indicate at this point the kind of criticism that has been made of Tillich's christology before proceeding to round it off with an exposition of his views on atonement. First of all, it has been pointed out that his attempts to save us from confusion about the historical Jesus have not been successful and that his contention that historical scepticism cannot harm faith presupposes a very peculiar view of historical truth. Then, several critics have commented on his actual christology and come to the conclusion that it is in the end inadequate. Some have argued that he has not substantiated his position that adoptionist and incarnational christologies are really interdependent. Others have contended that he cannot ensure a connection between the philosophical conception of 'eternal God-Manhood' and the concrete existence of the man Jesus. Questions have also been asked about the logical status of the concept 'the New Being' which seems in Tillich to be a universal principle and not a description of a concrete fact.

The Atonement

The atonement is the universal significance of Christ. This universal meaning is expressed by two central symbols which cor-

[28] *Ibid.*, p. 171.

respond to his subjection to existence and his conquest of its estrangement – the cross and the resurrection. These are interdependent symbols, and if separated they lose their meaning; for the cross is the cross of him who has 'conquered the death of existential estrangement', and the resurrection is the resurrection of him who 'as the Christ, subjected himself to the death of existential estrangement'. If the cross and the resurrection are interdependent then, says Tillich, 'they must be both reality and symbol'. In both cases there is a factual element or else it cannot be said that the Christ has entered existence and conquered it. But whereas the cross points to an event that probably took place in the clear light of history the resurrection-stories veil the event in mystery. In both cases, however, we also have a symbol – as the cross of Jesus who is the Christ, the cross 'is a symbol and a part of a myth',[29] and resurrection is a familiar mythological symbol. A real experience made it possible for the disciples to apply the symbol of resurrection to Jesus and so to acknowledge him definitely as the Christ.

If we ask what happened at the resurrection then we can answer, says Tillich, with some kind of historical conjecture. The most adequate theory, he thinks, is what he calls a 'restitution theory'. To understand what the resurrection is, he says, we must see what is overcome by it. 'The inactivity which is overcome in the resurrection is that of the disappearance of him whose being was the New Being.'[30] A tension was produced by the disciples' conviction that the power of his being was that of the New Being and their feeling that his disappearance was inconsistent with the character of the bearer of the New Being. In this tension something unique happened. 'In an ecstatic experience the concrete picture of Jesus of Nazareth became indissolubly united with the reality of the New Being.'[31] He is present wherever the New Being is present. He is 'the spirit' and 'we know him now' because he is in the spirit. This event happened first to some of his followers who had fled to Galilee in the hours of his execution; then to many others; then to Paul; then to all those who in every

[29] *Ibid.*, p. 177. [30] *Ibid.*, p. 181. [31] *Ibid.*, p. 181.

period experience his living presence here and now. This theory, Tillich however insists, is no more than a historical conjecture.

The universal significance of Jesus as the Christ can also be expressed in the term 'salvation'. There have been various interpretations of this in the history of Christianity, and according to Tillich in Roman Catholicism salvation is from guilt whilst in classical Protestantism it is from the law. Tillich himself understands it as meaning essentially 'healing', 'reuniting that which is estranged, giving a centre to that which is split, overcoming the split between God and man, and man and his world, man and himself'.[32] Just as there is a history of revelation, the centre of which is the event Jesus as the Christ, so the appearance of salvation through Christ is not separated from the processes of salvation which occur throughout all history. Indeed where there is revelation there too is salvation; for revelatory events are saving events in which the power of the New Being is present. That Jesus is the Saviour means, then, that he is the ultimate criterion of every saving process. Moreover, we need to realise that no distinction can be made between his person and his work. The doctrine of atonement is then the description of the effect of the New Being on those who are grasped by it in their state of estrangement. Atonement is both a divine act and a human reaction. It means the removal of human guilt as the factor responsible for man's separation from God, and this act of God is effective only in so far as man reacts and accepts the divine offer of reconciliation. Therefore, for Tillich, atonement necessarily has a subjective element, which introduces an indefiniteness into the doctrine. This is the reason, he thinks, why the church has refused to develop a dogma of the atonement similar to the dogma concerning the Person of Christ. Since there has been no dogma some radically different types of doctrine have been put forward. Two main types can be distinguished – the objective and the subjective. Tillich criticises the former as making atonement a cosmic drama which has no relation at all to man. This, he says, is not what the biblical objectivism means.[33] The subjective

[32] *Ibid.*, p. 192. [33] *Ibid.*, p. 198.

type of doctrine concerns itself with the liberating impression made upon men by the picture of Christ the crucified. The impression is that of his self-surrendering love which awakens in man an answering love which is convinced that God is ultimately love and not wrath. This theory does not satisfy Christian theology, says Tillich, because it ignores the need for justice in love.[34] Tillich takes an analogy from the psycho-analytic practice of inducing an abreaction in order to gain a catharsis. On the basis of this discussion of the types of atonement theory Tillich then offers six principles 'which should determine the further development of the doctrine of atonement'.[35]

1. The atoning processes are created by God and by God alone.
2. There are no conflicts between God's reconciling love and his retributive justice. Justice is the structural form of love without which love would be mere sentimentality.
3. The divine removal of guilt and punishment is not an act of overlooking the reality and depth of existential estrangement. God's forgiveness is no private matter.
4. God's atoning activity must be understood as his participation in existential estrangement and its self-destructive consequences.
5. In the cross of Christ the divine participation in existential estrangement becomes manifest. The cross of Christ is a manifestation 'by being actualisation'.
6. Through participation in the New Being, which is the being of Jesus as the Christ, men also participate in the manifestation of the atoning act of God.

The exposition of the soteriological aspects of Tillich's christology has been so lengthy that we can do no more than mention the criticisms that have been offered. It has been said that Tillich's emphasis on the subjective element in atonement leads him to distort the doctrine. The point can be put quite simply by saying that atonement cannot be reduced to either ethics or

[34] *Ibid.*, p. 199. [35] *Ibid.*, pp. 200–203.

psychology. Father G. H. Tavard probably speaks for others as well as himself when he says so vividly:

> Where the Council of Chalcedon, spearheading the Church, follows a ridge between two chasms, the Christology of Paul Tillich falls into both chasms one after the other.[36]

One of the most serious criticisms that have been made is that the discussion imperils the doctrine of the uniqueness of Christ's oblation of himself once offered.

The Doctrine of Man

More than once so far we have used the term 'existential estrangement' and now it is time to see what is involved in this description of the human situation. Tillich does not understand man's selfhood to be completely independent of the world. If we are to develop a doctrine of man, he says, we must start with man's self-relatedness which is the characteristic of all his experience. To be a self means that man is both over against the world and also in the world. Because of his self-consciousness man transcends his spatio-temporal environment, and yet he is also continuous with nature. The reciprocal relationship between 'personal' and 'communal' is a structural characteristic of being. Similarly freedom goes hand in hand with destiny. The structure of man's essential nature is the structure of finite freedom. The question of freedom should be raised as a question of element in man's ontological structure and not as the question of a faculty. The self is responsible, says Tillich, in so far as its acts are determined not by something external but 'by the centred totality of the person's being'.[37] It is the polarity of freedom and destiny that distinguishes human existence from other levels of existence; for the structure of man's essential nature is finite freedom. This concept of finitude is at the core of Tillich's doctrine of man and we have already seen how he sees it involved in the very idea of creation. The

[36] G. H. Tavard, *Paul Tillich and the Christian Message*, p. 132.
[37] *S.T.*, i, p. 204.

nihil in *creatio ex nihilo* describes, he says, the source of human nature. We come out of non-being. No doctrine of sin or of man's creatureliness can be adequate if it does not take account of non-being. When Augustine and others called sin 'non-being' they did not mean that sin had no reality but rather that sin has no positive ontological standing, while at the same time they understood 'non-being' as 'resistance to being' or 'perversion of being'. Man is created out of nothing and to nothing he must return. Being, limited by non-being, is finitude. To be something is to be finite, but finitude is experienced only by man. On the level of awareness finitude appears as anxiety, for finitude is the ontological basis of anxiety. Anxiety is not the same as fear, which has a definite object and can be eliminated by action. On the other hand, neither is anxiety the same as neurotic anxiety which results from inner conflicts. Anxiety is directed toward 'nothingness'. It is the self-awareness of the finite as finite, and as such has revealing power. As ontological, finitude characterises both the outward and the inner forms of experience.

The central category of finitude is time. Some philosophers have emphasised its negative element while others have called attention to its positive element. The former argue that the present is an illusion, that it is nothing more than a point moving from a non-existent past to a non-existent future. The philosophers who have emphasised the positive element of time have regarded time as creative, having an irreversible direction and ever producing something new. Neither of these analyses is satisfactory. Time cannot be illusory because being means being present; and if the present is an illusion then being is overcome by non-being. Neither can we say quite simply that time is creative because time not only creates but destroys what has been created. Corresponding to this paradox about the world outside us is the paradox about the inner world with its polarity between anxiety and courage. The onward march of time comes home to man in his anticipation of his own death, in his anxiety about *having* to die. This anxiety is potentially present in every moment and belongs to the created character of being. Now this natural anxiety is balanced by a courage which affirms temporarity. Indeed man is the most courageous of all beings because he has to conquer the deepest anxiety. Space is also implied by the present because 'the present always involves man's presence in it, and presence means having something present to one's self over against one's self'.[38] Like time, space unites being with non-being and anxiety with courage, and again like time, any discussion of space leads us to contradiction. Positively we may say that every being strives to maintain a 'place' for itself: 'to be' means to have space socially as well as physically. Yet, on the other hand, 'no finite being possesses a space which is definitely its own'.[39] and ultimately every place must be lost and with it being itself. This means ultimate insecurity and so anxiety. But this anxiety is balanced by the courage with which man affirms the present and, with it, space.[40]

Causality, like time and space, is ambiguous, expressing being and non-being.[41] Affirmatively, it points to the power from which things proceed, the power which can produce and maintain realities despite the resistance of non-being. On the other hand, however, finite things cannot be said to possess their own power of coming into being; they are 'thrown' into existence. The category of causality has its subjective counterpart in the polarity of human anxiety at our lack of self-sufficiency and the courage which achieves self-reliance despite the inescapable facts of contingency and dependence. The fourth category which describes this union of being and non-being in everything finite is substance.[42] Substance points to something underlying the flux of appearances. The concepts of substance and accidents are both logically and ontologically interdependent, and so 'in both substance and accidents the positive element is balanced by the negative element'. For men the concept of substance is related to the question of his self-identity. Traditionally, of course, the idea of the self is that of a substance. This idea arose out of discussions of the problem of survival, a question which expresses man's anxiety at the utter loss of his self-identity in death. This anxiety is answered

[38] *S.T.*, i, p. 216. [39] *Ibid.* [40] *Ibid.*, p. 217. [41] *Ibid.* [42] *Ibid.*, p. 218.

by the courage of affirming the finite – in the courage of a Keats who declares, 'I shall be amongst the immortals when I die.'

An obvious criticism of this discussion of finitude is that it depends on Tillich's interpretation of the formula *creatio ex nihilo*, an interpretation which is at least questionable. It is also objected that describing man's freedom as finite is to tell us nothing about this freedom except that it is not the same as God's. However, the most damaging criticism that has been made is that Tillich's idea of finitude can hardly be distinguished from his idea of sin. It has been said that, though Tillich has himself adequately formulated this objection – that sin may be a rational necessity, he does not answer it. To appreciate how this criticism could be made we must see how Tillich understands the nature of sin.

The Fall

The analysis of the human situation which he has offered is the analysis of those qualities which express the contrast between man's actual and his essential nature, and this for Tillich is the doctrine of the fall. This doctrine he describes as the transition from essence to existence. If we take the myth of Genesis 1–3 as a guide in the task of describing the transition from essential to existential being, we can discuss four things: (1) the possibility of the fall (2) its motives (3) the event itself (4) its consequences. How the fall is possible has in part been answered, Tillich thinks, by his discussion of the polarity of freedom and destiny and by the discussion of man's awareness of his own finitude and of finitude universally. The transition from essence to existence is possible only because of freedom which is in 'polar unity with destiny' and because man's freedom is finite. Man's freedom means that he has the power of contradicting himself and his essential nature. In the end, however, the transition from essence to existence is possible because finite freedom works within the framework of a universal destiny. Man's existence in the mythical paradise is to be interpreted psychologically as a state of 'dreaming innocence'. The state of dreaming innocence is driven forward by man's awareness of himself as finite. This awareness is 'anxiety'. So man's freedom is 'freedom in anxiety', or 'anxious freedom'. Two interrelated elements make up the motives of the transition from essence to existence – the divine prohibition and the anxious dilemma of man. 'The divine prohibition presupposes a kind of split between creator and creature, a split which makes a command necessary.'[43] This cleavage in turn presupposes a desire to sin. Man is caught between the desire to actualise his freedom and the demand to preserve his dreaming innocence. Thus he suffers the double anxiety of standing between the preservation of his dreaming innocence without experiencing the actuality of being and the loss of his innocence through knowledge, power and guilt. Man's decision in favour of self-actualisation brings dreaming innocence to an end. This transition from essence to existence, says Tillich, is the 'original fact' which 'gives validity to every fact'. That is to say, this is a universal quality of finite being. Naturally, therefore, Tillich insists that the doctrine of the fall has cosmic dimensions. The transition must be expressed by two kinds of myth – the myth of the transcendent fall and the myth of the immanent fall. In this way we emphasise both the tragic universality of sin as destiny and also its roots in ethical freedom. In this way Tillich tries to salvage the doctrine of original sin, a doctrine which has been under attack by modern man. It is the duty of the theologian, according to Tillich, to support the historical-critical attitude toward the biblical myth and the ecclesiastical myth and also to affirm the positive valuation of man's essential nature. As for the doctrine, however, he thinks it can be justified by the empirical evidence afforded by analytic psychology and sociology. These sciences have shown how destiny and freedom are interwoven in every human being.

Christian theology has always distinguished between original and actual sin, and Tillich accepts the distinction. As in the case of original sin so here he regards it as a matter of destiny, for the basic characteristic of sin is estrangement. He distinguishes three elements in sin[44] – unbelief, concupiscence and *hubris*. Unbelief is

[43] *S.T.*, ii, p. 40. [44] *Ibid.*, pp. 53–54.

what the Reformers understood by the term 'sin', and they defined 'unbelief' as 'an act of the total personality, including practical, theoretical and emotional elements'. For Protestant Christianity, therefore, sin means the separation of man's will from the will of God. Tillich rejects the concepts of disobedience and denial because he argues that these terms presuppose a separation from God. This definition of sin as unbelief need not, thinks Tillich, conflict with the Augustinian interpretation of sin as love turned away from God to self. Both emphasise the religious character of sin as indicating a relation between us and God. However, as against the Augustinian theory we must emphasise that sin is a matter of our relation to *God* and not to an ecclesiastical or any other authority. Tillich defines sin further by using the Greek tragic concept of *hubris* – 'the self-elevation of man into the sphere of the divine'.[45] This is not one form of sin, as the word, 'pride' in English suggests, but sin in its total form. It is the other side of unbelief. It is the turning toward one's self as the centre of one's self and one's world. Self-elevation characterises all human history, and all men have the hidden desire to be like God. Why should man be tempted to become centred in himself? The answer is that it places him in the position of drawing the whole of his world into himself. Every individual wants abundance, and the possibility of reaching unlimited abundance is the temptation of man. The classical name for this desire is concupiscence – 'the unlimited desire to draw the whole of reality into one's self'.[46] Neither the identification of this desire with sexual appetite nor Nietzsche's 'will to power' nor again Freud's 'libido' is an adequate interpretation of concupiscence. It is an unlimited desire. As we saw above, Tillich insists that sin is a universal fact before it becomes an individual act. This does not mean that he holds any view of collective guilt. There is no such thing, he says, though he admits that individual guilt helps to create the universal destiny of mankind.

On the question of immortality, too, Tillich finds Genesis enlightening. In the story man is created from dust and will return

[45] *Ibid.*, p. 57. [46] *Ibid.*, p. 59.

to dust. He has immortality only as long as he is allowed to eat of the fruit of the tree of life. This Tillich interprets as a symbolical assertion of the fact that 'participation in the eternal makes man eternal'. Sin is not the cause of death but what gives death the power which is conquered only by 'participation in the eternal'. Sin transforms the anxious awareness of one's having to die into the painful realisation of a lost eternity. This shows how anxious Tillich is to preserve intact the distinction between finitude and sin.

Church and Sacraments

We have seen how the New Being overcomes existential estrangement, but it will be recalled that Jesus is the Christ, the bearer of the New Being in so far as he is thus received. The community in which Jesus is received as the Christ is the church, the 'assembly of God' or of the Christ. This church is the historical continuation of the 'chosen race' of the Old Testament. Jesus' calling of the twelve apostles indicates his messianic purpose of collecting the true people of God. The church is, then, the community of those who are called out of all nations by the good news proclaimed by the apostles. The church is founded by its reception of Jesus as the Christ. This is not a matter of history but the work of the divine spirit. This is what is mythically expressed by the common assertion that the church began at Pentecost. This spiritual foundation of the church is not to be understood deistically. It is the New Being in Jesus as the Christ being actualised as community by the creative power of the divine spirit through word and sacrament.

The word is the main instrument in the foundation of the church. When the divine spirit works through the human word this word becomes the 'Word of God.'[47] What makes the word, then, the word of God is both its content and its being word of God for somebody. Even the biblical word is 'Word of God' in so far as the spirit bears witness to it. Every word can become the

[47] *S.T.*, iii, p. 132.

vehicle of the divine spirit in a special situation, but the criterion is always the word become flesh, the New Being in Jesus as the Christ. The church is founded by sacrament as well as word because of the unity of man's spirituality with his vitality. This makes sensuous instruments necessary in the church's foundation; and the action of the divine spirit through them makes these instruments sacramental objects. What makes the sacraments significant in the life of the church is their spiritual effect which concerns man's spiritual life both consciously and subconsciously. In our attempts at understanding this effect we must avoid both magical interpretation and over-intellectual interpretations. The sacramental materials are for Tillich symbols, and in this connection we recall that he has argued that symbols are to be distinguished from signs. So with regard to the sacramental materials he says that the Catholic doctrine of transubstantiation transforms a symbol into a thing to be handled and the Reformed doctrine reduces the sacramental symbol to a sign. 'A sacramental symbol is neither a thing nor a sign. It participates in the power of what it symbolises, and therefore, it can be the medium of the spirit.'[48] The particular sacraments of the church have no more biblical foundation than they have a foundation in systematic theology. The reasons for their selection are those of tradition, practical evaluation and criticism of abuses. Usually they arise either in connection with great moments in the individual's life (such as birth, maturity, marriage and imminent death) or with special religious events or – most characteristically – with the ritual activities of the group itself. Word and sacrament should not be separated. Christ as the word of God is both word and sacrament, and their unity in him means that they should also be united in his church.

The church is the New Being as community – the community of faith and love. As the community of faith the church receives the New Being in Christ as its foundation and its life-principle. This means that for the individual there is a decision to be made – whether or not he wishes to belong to a community which

[48] *Ibid.*, p. 131.

asserts that Jesus is the Christ. If he decides against this he has left the church whether or not in fact he ceases to belong to a particular church. The problem of heresy arises when the conceptual formulation of the implications of the basic Christian assertion is undertaken. Tillich does not think that the word 'heresy' should be saved though he admits that the problem to which it points is unavoidable.[49] The problem is solved, he thinks, if we recognise that 'the Protestant principle of the infinite distance between the divine and the human undercuts the absolute claim of any doctrinal expression of the New Being'.[50] As well as being a community of faith the churches are also a community of love, but this too must be understood within the ambiguities of religion and of the spirit's struggle with these ambiguities. As the community of love the church actualises the spiritual community which is its essence. Because of this the church is the place of equality – that is, equality before God. This does not necessarily imply social or political equality, even within the church itself, but it does necessarily imply the rejection of any form of inequality as destructive of the community of faith and love. Again, the church as community of love is the agent of charity toward everyone in need both inside and outside its fold. This does not necessarily involve the creation of economic equality but does reject any kind of individualism which uses charity as a means of maintaining the evils of a *status quo*.

It is clear that for Tillich the church must not be regarded as above the ambiguities of social existence. Indeed he insists that every church is a sociological reality. As such it is subject to the laws which determine the life of social groups with all their ambiguities.[51] Sociological principles about the rise and fall of élites are as easily discerned in this society as in any other. Judging the churches from the point of view of their sociological function and their social influence, past or present, is utterly inadequate. The other view of the churches is the theological. This does not refuse to admit the sociological aspect but it points 'within the ambiguities of the social reality of the churches, to the presence

[49] *Ibid.*, p. 188. [50] *Ibid.*, pp. 188–89. [51] *Ibid.*, p. 176.

of the unambiguous spiritual community'.[52] But, just as in the case of the sociological view it was wrong to interpret the church exclusively in its terms so too with regard to the theological view. The error of Roman Catholicism and of some forms of Protestantism, Tillich points out, is that this paradoxical character of the churches is denied. Both Catholicism and Protestantism negate the paradox that the theological nature of the church is actual in and through its sociological nature. Tillich applies this paradox in two ways. First he argues that the paradox is revealed in the fact that the attributes of the spiritual community are taken as marks of the churches – holiness, unity and universality. Secondly, the paradox of the churches leads him to reject any suggestion that there exists an invisible church alongside the visible. It will be easier to expound the second point first. Tillich has come completely to avoid the use of the term 'the church', and when he talks of the body of Christ he uses the term 'spiritual community'.[53] The Reformers' distinction between the 'church visible' and the 'church invisible' has been misunderstood so that the latter is understood as a reality alongside the church visible. Such a misunderstanding is in fact a devaluation of the empirical church; for the invisible church is 'the spiritual essence of the visible church'. Tillich warns against two mistakes which can so easily be made. The one is the interpretation of the spiritual community as an ideal toward which the churches are steadily moving. Against this it is necessary to affirm that the church as the body of Christ is the New Creation into which the individual Christian and the particular church is taken. The other danger to be avoided is a mythological literalism according to which the spiritual community is an assembly of so-called spiritual beings. But this is not the spiritual community, and it calls for a category pointing to the power of the essential behind and within the existential.

The paradox of the churches is further seen in the fact that the attributes of the spiritual community are those ascribed to the empirical church. Each of these attributes – holiness, unity and

[52] *Ibid.*, p. 177. [53] *Ibid.*, p. 174.

universality – cannot be ascribed to the churches without some proviso. Thus we can say that the churches are holy in spite of the actual unholiness of their members. 'The holiness of the churches and of Christians is not a matter of empirical judgment but rather of faith in the working of the New Being within them.'[54] The churches are holy because they stand under 'the negative and positive judgments of the cross'. This is where Protestant and Catholic doctrines of the church seem irreconcilable, and Tillich raises the question of how far the kind of reformation which has been witnessed in contemporary Catholicism can go. However, part of what is meant by the churches' holiness is that they have the principle of reformation within themselves because as long as they are churches the spiritual presence works in them. In his exposition of the second of the churches' characteristics – unity – Tillich speaks of the churches as united[55] rather than of their being one. They are so united because of the unity of their foundation, the New Being. As with their holiness he insists that the unity of the churches can no more be derived from their actual unity than it can be contradicted by their actual disunity. The predicate, he says, 'is identical with the dependence of any actual church on the spiritual community as its essence in power and structure'.[56] Any church, then, which is so related to the event of the Christ displays the unity of the church, and this unity is real in them in spite of the fact that all of them are separated from each other. It is the divided church, then, which is for Tillich the united church, and this, he recognises, is an essentially Protestant position which the Roman Catholic Church could only accept if it gave up its absolute claim. Finally, the paradox of the nature of the churches is revealed by their universality. They are universal because of the universality of their foundation, the New Being. Though he avoids the use of the word 'catholic' Tillich insists that 'a church which does not claim catholicity has ceased to be a church'.[57] He distinguishes between the intensive and extensive universality of

[54] *Ibid.*, p. 179.
[55] *Ibid.*, p. 180.
[56] *Ibid.*, p. 180.
[57] *Ibid.*, p. 181.

the church. The former is 'its power and desire to participate as church in everything created under all dimensions of life'.[58] This does not mean a simple identification of the church and the world, for Tillich recognises the church will have to judge and fight against the ambiguities of life which it meets. It does, however, mean that the church is essentially an open society, open to the whole of creation. This is the meaning of the *complexio oppositorum* of which the Roman Church is 'rightly proud'. The danger which this involved was that ambiguity entered the very life of the church, and this led Protestantism to replace the abundance of this principle by the poverty of sacred emptiness.[59] Even here, however, the principle of universality is not violated; for there can be a universality of emptiness as well as a universality of abundance. 'Yet, however positive or negative the churches' attitude toward the predicate of universality, they are essentially universal in spite of their actual poverty in relation to the abundance of the encountered world.'[60] All that has been said of the churches' intensive universality can equally be said of their extensive universality – the validity of the church's foundation for all nations, social groups, races, tribes and cultures. Yet there is never an actual universality in the churches which would make the predicate of universality a matter of empirical fact. The extensive or (if I may so describe it) the concrete universality of the churches is a paradoxical predicate like their intensive universality. Tillich does not seem to entertain any high hopes of there ever being actual universality of the churches. The idea that 'one day in the future these predicates will lose their paradoxical character and become empirically true' he dismisses as 'utopian expectations'.[61]

If this is the essential nature of the churches what of their functions? Three groups of church functions can be distinguished: 'the functions of constitution, related to the foundation of the churches in the spiritual community; the functions of expansion, related to the universal claim of the spiritual community; the functions of construction, related to the actualisation of the

[58] *Ibid.* [59] *Ibid.*, p. 182. [60] *Ibid.* [61] *Ibid.*, p. 186.

spiritual potentialities of the churches'.[62] All these functions bear the mark of the churches' paradox. Involved in the ambiguity of life they aim to conquer these ambiguities through the power of the spiritual presence. As well as distinguishing functions Tillich distinguishes the polarities corresponding to them. Thus the functions of constitution stand under the polarity of tradition and reformation. By tradition Tillich does not mean simply the sociological fact of the dependence of any culture on that of the preceding generation but also the fact that there is some link between the foundation of the churches in Jesus as the Christ and every new generation. Tradition, he says, 'is not particular, although it includes all particular traditions; it expresses the unity of historical mankind of which the appearance of the Christ is the centre'.[63] The term 'Reformation' is used in two senses. It indicates the historical event of the Protestant Reformation and it signifies 'a permanent principle, active in all periods, which is implied in the spirit's fight against the ambiguities of religion'.[64] A movement of Reformation has no objective criterion but always, by the courage of the prophetic spirit, faces risk; and it faces the risk in the certain faith that nothing can destroy the spiritual community. Corresponding to the function of expansion in the life of the churches is the polarity of the principles of verity and adaptation. The problem is as old as the New Testament where its classical expression is in Paul who both describes himself as a Jew to the Jews and a Greek to the Greeks and rejects everyone who tries to transform the gospel into Jewish law or Greek wisdom. Verity without adaptation leads, says Tillich, to 'a demonic absolutism which throws the truth like stones at the heads of people, not caring whether they can accept it or not'.[65] On the other hand, the danger of adaptation is that it becomes an unlimited accommodation so that the verity of the message is lost and the church becomes relativist, which leads to secularism. Finally, corresponding to the functions of construction is the polarity of the principles of form-transcendence and form-affirmation. The functions of construction use materials which

[62] *Ibid.*, p. 195. [63] *Ibid.*, p. 196. [64] *Ibid.*, p. 197. [65] *Ibid.*, p. 199.

are drawn from all the various areas of cultural creation in order to express the spiritual community in the life of the churches. This they do as churches, according to Tillich, 'only if the relation of the spiritual presence is manifest in their works, and this means if there is an ecstatic form-transcending quality in them'.[66] On the other hand, the church cannot use the cultural form in any old way. 'In every function of the church the essential form of the cultural realm must be used without a violation of its structural demands.'[67] Tillich relates this to what he has said earlier in the system about structure and ecstasy, but it seems to be quite a straightforward point. What he is insisting on here is the necessity for the church to be faithful both to her own essentially theological nature and to the demands of whatever culture she employs in the course of her constructive task. That is to say, neither will piety make up for feeble or bastardised culture nor will a brilliant culture make up for lack of Christian faith. The business of the church is to work with the tension created by these demands, and where the spiritual presence is abundantly manifest the two principles are united. If these are the functions of the church, it might be asked, who performs these functions? Are they performed by a priest? Tillich clearly and emphatically advocates a priesthood of all believers. In so far as anyone belongs actively to a church he is a priest. However, he is prepared to admit that 'for the sake of order and adequacy to the situation, special individuals may be called to a regular and trained performance of priestly duties'.[68]

There has not been very much criticism of Tillich's views on the church because these views were expounded only in the third volume of *Systematic Theology*. A Catholic theologian has argued that Tillich's zeal for God's transcendence has led him unnecessarily to oppose the authority claimed by the Roman Church and further that this makes him take the curious position of denying to God the freedom he allows to man.[69] Other criticisms are that Tillich's constant use of paradox is unhelpful, that the distinc-

[66] *Ibid.*, pp. 199–200. [67] *Ibid.*, p. 200. [68] *Ibid.*, p. 231.
[69] E. O'Connor, 'Paul Tillich: An Impression,' in *Thought*, 1955, pp. 507 ff.

tions he makes between the church manifest and the church latent is unnecessary in so far as it says no more than that there is a preparation for the gospel, and finally that Tillich's doctrine of the church is inadequate because he rejects any principle of scriptural authority in the church.

History and the Kingdom of God

The final part of Tillich's system is a theological discussion of history which, he says, deals with 'the structure of historical processes, the logic of historical knowledge, the ambiguities of historical existence, the meaning of the historical movement', and it must 'relate all this to the symbol of the kingdom of God, both in its inner-historical and its trans-historical sense'.[70] Dealing with the nature of history Tillich begins by distinguishing two senses – the subjective and the objective. These are made clear to us by the development of the Greek word *historia* from meaning primarily inquiry or report to its use as meaning the events inquired about and reported. There is no history without factual occurrences and there is no history without 'the reception and interpretation of factual occurrences by historical consciousness'.[71] Tillich seems to feel that he solves the problem of the subject-object character of history by defining event as a syndrome of facts and interpretation. This dual character is found, he says, in all historical events properly so-called. The characteristics of history are: 'to be connected with purpose, to be influenced by freedom, to create the new in terms of meaning, to be significant in a universal, particular and theological sense'.[72] In some ways, at least, Tillich is repeating the analysis of history which he gave in his *The Interpretation of History* where he insists that history exists only where there is decision and that individual events are the subject of historical research. Another feature which the analyses have in common is their interpretation of the meaning of history as being necessarily teleological. This analysis distinguishes

[70] *S.T.*, iii, p. 318. [71] *Ibid.*
[72] *Ibid.*, p. 325. Cf. pp. 323 ff.

between the history of man which is, by definition, the only real history and the historical dimension in general. One can find an analogy to history in the spontaneity of nature, but in all realms other than human history, history remains 'an anticipated, but unactualised, dimension'. 'The development from anticipated to actual history can be described as the state of prehistorical man.'[73] The subject of history is human individuals and groups, though the direct bearers of history are groups rather than individuals, who are only indirect bearers. The characteristics of a history-bearing group are, first, that it should be able to act 'in a centred way' and this means that it must have 'a central law-giving, administering and enforcing authority'. These are the characteristics of a state, and so the history of historical groups is the history of states. Tillich does not mean to say that there is such a thing as a historical group alongside individuals but simply that an individual is 'a bearer of history only in relation to history-bearing group'.[74] Biography, he says, is not history and can only become significant either as the story of someone who represents a group or as the account of an individual who is typical of a situation within the group. The central category of history is that of time, and historical time involves physical or inorganic time while the latter provides only a basis for history. The characteristic of historical time is irreversibility. 'Under no dimension does time go backward . . . Time, so to speak, runs ahead toward the new, the unique, the novel, even in repetitions.'[75] There can be no time without space and so there is no historical time without historical space. Historical time is actual in the relations of historical spaces. 'As in historical time the meaning of after-each-otherness is raised to consciousness and has become a human problem, so in historical space the meaning of beside-each-otherness is raised to consciousness and has also become a problem. The answer in both cases is identical with the answer to the question of the aim of the historical process.'[76] Tillich completes this categorical analysis of history with a description of historical situation as the substance in history and some remarks on historical causality as

[73] *Ibid.*, p. 326. [74] *Ibid.*, p. 333. [75] *Ibid.*, p. 340. [76] *Ibid.*, p. 342.

future-directed.[77] This analysis leads him to distinguish as the basic elements of a description of the movement of history the following: the irreversibility of historical movement (from time), freedom (from causality), the relatively static element (from space and substance). Though Tillich continues this analysis of the concept of history with a discussion of the dynamics of history and the ambiguities of life before coming to the problem of an interpretation of history we can come directly to this as the central point in his theology of history.

Tillich defines his problem as the question: What is the significance of history for the meaning of existence in general? With the definition of this question there arises another problem – namely, how can we find an answer to this question? The subject-object character of history makes an objective – that is to say, detached, or scientific – answer impossible. 'Only full involvement in historical action can give the basis for an interpretation of history. Historical activity is the key to understanding history.'[78] The question that arises then is which type of historical activity provides the right key. Tillich answers this question by reminding us that theology moves within the theological circle and so the answer is in a sense already given by our very undertaking. This answer is the Christian conviction that there is a direction to history, what Tillich calls the Christian vocational consciousness. 'In the Christian vocational consciousness, history is affirmed in such a way that the problems implied in the ambiguities of life under the dimension of history are answered through the symbol "kingdom of God".'[79] This does not mean, however, that we need no further argument about the meaning of history. On the contrary, Tillich thinks that we need to test this assertion by contrasting the symbol 'kingdom of God' with the other main types of interpretation and then to reinterpret the symbol in the light of these contrasts. The biblical source of this interpretation of history is clear enough. Tillich conceives history as being always crisis in much the same way as the Old Testament

[77] See *ibid.*, pp. 346–47.

[78] *Ibid.*, pp. 372–73.

[79] *Ibid.*, p. 373.

prophets did. It is under judgment and it is crisis in the sense of having an aim toward which it is moving.

He talks of the dissatisfaction which the religious Socialists of the 1920's (and here the group surely symbolises the individual) felt with the progressivistic, utopian and transcendental interpretations of history. This dissatisfaction led them, he says,[80] to try a solution which is based on biblical prophetism in terms of a re-interpretation of the symbol of the kingdom of God. The kingdom of God 'has an inner-historical and a transhistorical side', embracing everything in the course of history as its transcendent meaning while yet naming the ultimate fulfilment intended in history. The symbol has four characteristics – it is political, social, personalistic and universal.[81] That the symbol is political in character is appropriate because, as we have seen, the political sphere predominates in the dynamics of history. Tillich does not tell us much about the political character of the symbol but contents himself with pointing out that there is no particular kind of political view here used – 'king' has always been, he says, a symbol of the highest and the most consecrated centre of political control. The social character of the symbol indicates the significance of justice and of personality and personal relationships for the ultimate fulfilment. This constantly reminds us that there is no holiness without the unconditional moral imperative of justice. The third characteristic is that the kingdom of God gives eternal meaning to the individual person, and its transhistorical aim is not the extinction but the fulfilment of the individual. Finally, the kingdom of God is not only a kingdom of men but the fulfilment of life under all dimensions. The kingdom of God expresses the ultimate fulfilment in which the contrast between essence and existence is overcome universally and completely. The appearance of the New Being in whom this contrast is overcome constitutes the centre of history, and in Christ as the centre of history the kingdom of God manifests itself as the ultimate meaning of history. This, says Tillich, is a critique of both relativism and progressivism.[82] The manifestation of the kingdom of God in

[80] *Ibid.*, p. 381. [81] *Ibid.*, pp. 382 ff. [82] *Ibid.*, p. 389.

history is not an incoherent series of manifestations and, as manifestation of the centre of history, it implies that there is no progress beyond it. This is the only event in which the historical dimension as such is fulfilled. This moment of maturity at which there was the decisive 'breakthrough of the central manifestation of the kingdom of God'[83] is what is called in the New Testament *kairos,* and this is the central idea in Tillich's interpretation of history. He first used the term *kairos* in philosophical and theological discussions connected with the religious Socialist movement in Germany after the First World War. His intention was to find some third alternative to or compromise between Socialist utopianism and Lutheran transcendentalism. One of the things he wanted to express by means of this term was the feeling that a 'moment of history had appeared which was pregnant with a new understanding of the meaning of history and life'.[84] Originally the term *kairos* is contrasted with the other Greek word for time, *chronos*: the former is qualitative whereas the latter is quantitative. It is the distinction between the time of fulfilment and the time that is measured. As well as the particular use of the term in the New Testament to denote the time of the coming of Christ Tillich thinks there can be a more general use. So he talks of the experience of a *kairos* occurring again and again in the history of the churches. '*Kairoi* have occurred and are occurring in all preparatory and receiving movements in the church latent and manifest.'[85] *Kairoi* can be demonically distorted and they can be erroneous. The former is a fact only too evident to the twentieth century. But how can the *kairos* be erroneous? The answer is that it is not the *kairos* that is in error but the judgment about its character in terms of the facts of the world. Are there then any periods in history in which no *kairos* is experienced? Tillich's answer is that whereas obviously the kingdom of God and the Spiritual Presence are never absent in any moment of time the experience of the kingdom's presence as determining history is not always given.[86]

The symbol of the kingdom of God indicates the fulfilment of

[83] *Ibid.*, p. 393. [84] *Ibid.*, p. 394. [85] *Ibid.*, p. 395. [86] *Ibid.*, p. 396.

history. The kingdom does not belong entirely to another world: the churches are the representatives of the kingdom of God. 'As representatives of the kingdom of God, the churches share actively both in the running of historical time toward the aim of history and in the inner-historical struggle of the kingdom of God against the forces of demonisation and profanisation that fight against this aim.'[87] Tillich warns against the identification of the churches with the kingdom of God. One thing is quite obvious, he says, that is that one cannot call church history 'sacred history' or a 'history of salvation'.[88] Church history is capable of self-judgment because it is related to the New Being, and because of this relation it is also able to judge the history of the world. So we can discern in history the fragmentary victories of the kingdom of God which point to the non-fragmentary side of the kingdom of God 'above' history which is the 'end' of history.[89]

[87] *Ibid.*, p. 407. [88] *Ibidem.* [89] *Ibid.*, p. 420.

3

Significance

Now that we have sketched an outline of Tillich's theology we can appreciate that there is no single answer to the question, What makes Tillich important? Indeed the very complexity of Tillich's system is for many people symptomatic of the difficulty they find in his thought. It needs to be said that this kind of bewilderment is justifiable and that Tillich is not only difficult but often obscure. Then again the novelty of what he has said on many topics has caused many people to forget that the clue to what Tillich means is very often found only when we have struggled to discover his sources. Similarly because we are so sure that Tillich is a great theologian we are in danger of treating him in the same way as we treat great artists, showing him that uncritical devotion for which anything the artist does is excellent. For too many people it is axiomatic that what Paul Tillich says is true. This is not, however, the kind of debt which he envisages himself laying upon us, since for him his theological system is simply a help in answering questions. If any simple answer is then to be given to our question, What makes Tillich important? it is that he has forced us to ask certain basic questions about theology which we need to ask and he has shown the kind of courage we need to answer them. What kind of questions these are we must now try to make clear.

Theology and the Modern Situation

Tillich's theology is radical in the sense that it has tried to get down to fundamental issues. Thus he begins by trying to explain what theology is. If anyone feels that this is a negative attitude for a theologian to take he will be surprised at his positive doctrine that theology is the rational effort to unite humanly and organically the data of revelation. There is nothing trivial about this conception of theology's task. In the last analysis revelation is, says Tillich, something received only externally and so the content of revelation must be sought not only in the history of doctrine or in scripture but also in the cultural postulates of communities. The method that theology must employ is the method of correlation because in theology the unforgivable sin (and the ever-present temptation) is irrelevance. Tillich has striven to be relevant and contemporary. It has been said that he has failed in this, but that this was his intention no one has denied. So he has been hailed as the theological prophet of our time. In view of the fact that theologians like Barth and Niebuhr seem to be speaking with a voice more like that of the biblical prophets we might be led to wonder whether we now prefer prophets who do not have a biblical voice. Be that as it may there are several points in Tillich's thought where his feeling for the contemporary situation is clear enough. It may not be true that Tillich has spoken to modern man with a penetration that has not been equalled by anyone else, but it is true that it is to modern man in all his meaninglessness that he has addressed his theology. Also it may be that the honesty he has displayed in his theological reflections has been the most important reason why people have seen in him one who did interpret the traditional message in their terms. If this is not so then it is extremely difficult to understand why people accord the title of 'modern theologian' to one whose outlook is so clearly that of the nineteenth century. The use of words like 'meaninglessness' or phrases like 'the disintegration of traditional values' is not enough to warrant the claim that Tillich has presented a theological analysis of the modern situation. He has indeed described himself as an existentialist philosopher, a title which is still regarded by many as the most modern title a philosopher can bear, and it is true that he has been profoundly influenced by some modern philosophers such as Heidegger. However, the influence of those philosophers who in the nineteenth century blazed the trail, along which Heidegger and others have since travelled, is much more important. It may be that Tillich's modernity is much more a matter of mood than intellectual standpoint or even terminology. Certainly when one turns to more ecclesiastical concerns he seems to express the mood of modern Christendom in his contention that there is now a *kairos*, a moment full of potentialities, in Protestant–Catholic relations. Nor is this simply a matter of ecclesiology; for Tillich's whole work is characterised by his attempt to unite the protestant principle with the substance of the Catholic faith. He is at once thoroughly Protestant and yet so open to the appeal of Catholicism. For him neither the 'sacramental' principle of Catholicism nor the 'prophetic' principle of Protestantism can stand on its own. Therefore, inevitable though it may be that institutional Catholicism and institutional Protestantism will clash, there is, he thinks, no essential clash between the two principles. They are complementary elements of the true 'theonomous' Christianity. Toward the end of *Systematic Theology* he says:

> The Protestant principle is an expression of the conquest of religion by the spiritual presence and consequently an expression of the victory over the ambiguities of religion, its profanisation, its denomination. It is Protestant because it protests against the magic-demonic self-elevation of religion. . . . It alone is not enough; it needs the 'Catholic substance', the concrete embodiment of the spiritual presence; but it is the criterion of the demonisation (and profanisation) of such embodiment. It is the expression of the victory of the spirit over religion.[90]

Tillich has not himself either played a very important rôle in the ecumenical movement or even entertained very sanguine hopes for the movement. So it may be that those who have hoped for a theology of the ecumenical movement from Tillich will be disappointed. The final volume of *Systematic Theology* does not offer us a blueprint for healing 'our unhappy divisions' and can be said to advance the ecclesiological debate very little. Yet in so far as he has expressed the mood of expectancy and impatience

[90] *S.T.*, iii, p. 245.

with merely one-sided answers Tillich has spoken with the authentic voice of the twentieth century.

Theology and Metaphysics

Another answer to our question was suggested by Reinhold Niebuhr in his contribution to the *Theology of Paul Tillich* when he says that 'Tillich's greatness lies in his exploration of the boundary between metaphysics and theology'.[91] For those who have been influenced by the revolution in English philosophy this claim seems not too well-founded. There is for Tillich only one philosophy – the more traditional kind which is symbolised for most people by that great unkown of modern philosophy – Hegel. Certainly Tillich's philosophical outlook is very close to the Idealism which dominated the nineteenth century, if not to Hegel, whose influence can without doubt be discerned, then clearly to Schelling. He prides himself on perpetuating a Platonic tradition in philosophy and it is not difficult to pick out examples of the influence which medieval Platonism exerted on him. His knowledge of the history of philosophy is a byword in American theology. Now this kind of openness to the past may have been missing from a good deal of contemporary philosophy; but this has not meant that Tillich was really any less likely to go astray. Indeed his strength is also his weakness. He has not seen that metaphysics must suffer a sea-change into something no less rich for being strange. The progress of philosophy away from the anti-metaphysical bias of Logical Positivism and some linguistic philosophy toward a more metaphysical inquiry has made us appreciate Tillich's strength as a philosophical theologian.

This positive appraisal of Tillich will give him credit for recognising the place of mystery in any adequate philosophy. As we have seen, Tillich stands in a tradition of romantic philosophy and thus he has inherited much of the content as well as the language of German mysticism. His inspiration was Schelling and it was probably through him that he became familiar with

[91] *Op. cit.*, p. 226.

the cobbler-mystic, Jacob Boehme. The references to Boehme in *Systematic Theology* are evidence enough of Tillich's high estimate of Boehme's 'metaphysical-psychological' description of the living God. Some philosophers have been quite contemptuous in their references to Tillich's work. Contempt, no more than uncritical admiration, will not enable us to do theology better; and I believe that if we approach Tillich with a critical mind we shall learn a good deal. We shall learn that it is not enough to avow theology's relations with philosophy – we must show them in action. There is a point indeed at which Tillich does precisely this. His analysis of revelation shows the concern of theology with epistemological issues far better than his formal correlation of philosophy and theology. Too often, however, he side-steps basic issues so that he appears less a metaphysician militant or even triumphant than a metaphysician manqué.

Theology and Culture

Finally, Tillich has been described as one of the few theologians of culture. This has been an important direction for his thinking ever since the earliest days of his academic career. As a student he loved poetry and philosophy no less than theology, and as a professional teacher of philosophy he was concerned to make his students think out with him a theology of culture. His whole life has been filled with a passion for those aesthetic values which transcend any one discipline and which effect a correlation between disciplines. More than any other living theologian probably he has shown himself sensitive to sociology and psychology and above all to art. His discovery of painting he has called an experience of decisive importance; for here he was able to penetrate that mysterious world on the boundary between reality and imagination. His aim, in short, was to try to integrate all the fields of human creativity and experience. Sociology had, in a sense, always been Tillich's concern. He tells us that he had lived on the boundary between social classes: though born a member of the bourgeoisie he had never become bourgeois because he had contact both with the old nobility and the lower classes. But it was the First World War which contributed the sociological dimension to his theology. He was, he says, 'grasped by the overwhelming experience of a nationwide community – of the end of a merely individualistic and predominantly theoretical existence'.[92] Returning from the war he was shocked by the irrelevance of so much Christian preaching and teaching and this led him to support the Socialist movement which was then making itself felt in German politics. He was never a party-man, but it is not too much to say that his work at this period was an attempt at supplying the theological justification for the social reshaping which was the aim of Socialism. Many years later he was to say that any real expression in politics of the prophetic message of justice should be called religious Socialism. Some of Tillich's more recent work (such as *Love, Power and Justice*) reveal that this interest in politics is still very much alive, while his sociological analysis of American history in *The Courage to Be* must strike many of us as the most illuminating outline of the American tradition that we have read. Again, his more formally theological discussions (such as that of the nature of sin in *Systematic Theology*, ii, and that of the nature of the church in iii) show an equal readiness to learn what sociology has to teach.

Psychology too has been a field to whose borders he has brought his theology. He has used psychological ideas in his discussion of the doctrine of original sin and in the analysis he has himself offered of the concept of sin. Thus he effects a very illuminating translation of the mythological expression of original sin into psychological terms and he is quite prepared to borrow psychological theories to support what he has to say about concupiscence. Both theoretically and practically, psychology is for Tillich one of the most instructive teachers the theologian can find. It can teach him something about the nature of man and even about the nature of the new situation in which God's grace puts him. Just as the psychologist's patient has to learn to accept himself so the Christian has to accept the fact that

[92] *The Theology of Paul Tillich*, p. 12.

he is accepted. Here, as we say, Tillich finds a clue to understanding the mystery of atonement. Nor is this borderline activity one in which theology alone can profit. Psychology, thinks Tillich, has something to learn from theology – e.g. the distinction between pathological anxiety and a more fundamental religious anxiety about the perpetual threat of the meaninglessness of existence. Man's basic disorder can be remedied only by a theonomous psychology, a co-operative effort of psychology and religion.

Perhaps it is Tillich's readiness to see a religious value in all kinds of art that makes him so important and impressive as a theologian of culture. His famous essay on a theology of culture expounds his view that religion is the substance of culture and culture is the expression of religion. Art expresses man's spiritual aspirations and insights. Tillich seeks the unity of culture which will mirror the unity of the real. He has been ready to learn all that art can reveal to him. The expressionist movement exerted a strong influence on him and he has not been slow to point out the lessons of existentialist art for the theologian.[93] At a time when the greatest need of theology is to pay attention to what the artists reveal about the broken culture of our modern rootless world these are solid achievements.

Paul Tillich is a difficult theologian, but he repays critical reading. If some of the popularity he has recently gained has been due to the rash employment of some of his more obscure ideas it is to be hoped that a fuller and more informed understanding of his thought will issue in clearer and richer theology.

[93] See *The Courage to Be*, pp. 136–40.